Beginner's Guide to
MOSAICS

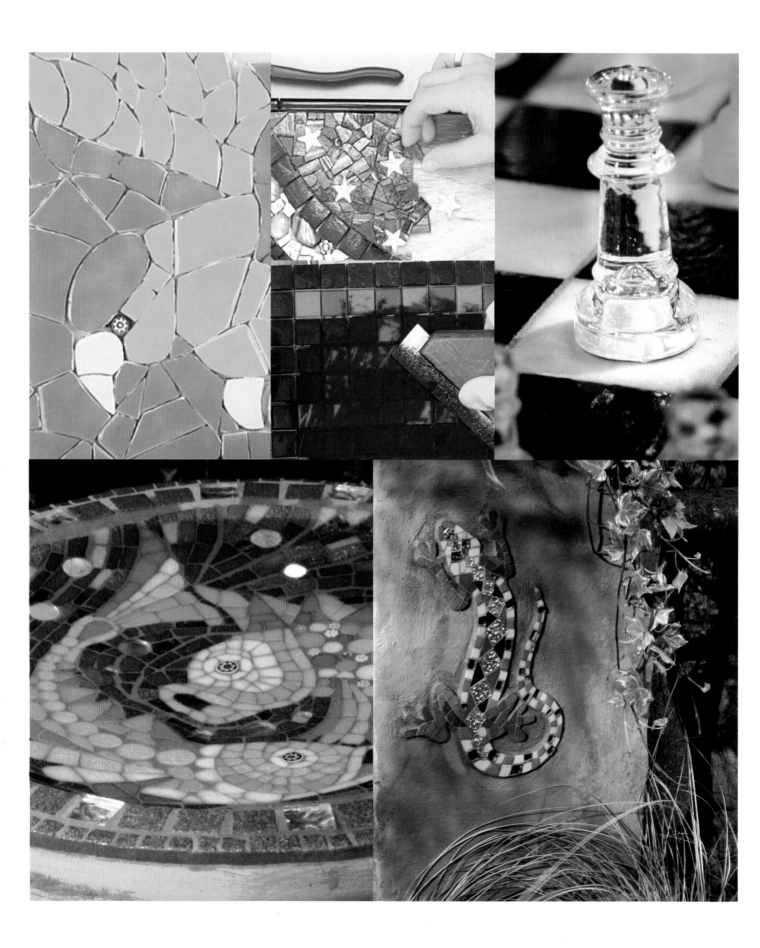

Beginner's Guide to
MOSAICS

ALISON HEPBURN

Sterling Publishing Co., Inc.
New York

Creative director: Sarah King
Project editor: Anna Southgate
Designer: 2H Design

Library of Congress Cataloging-in-Publication Data

10   9   8   7   6   5   4   3   2   1

This edition published in 2005 by Sterling Publishing Co.,Inc.
387 Park Avenue South,
New York, N.Y. 10016

© 2003 D&S Books Ltd

Distributed in Canada by Sterling Publishing
c/o Canadian Manda Group,
165 Dufferin Street Toronto,
Ontario, Canada M6K 3H6

Printed in China

Sterling ISBN 1-4027-2841-7

Contents

Introduction

Like many people, my first experience of mosaic was in swimming pools and shop doorways. I was captivated by the colors, the texture, and the intricacy, which made me long to see more without any real idea of where to look. Fans and creators of mosaic range from international artists to school children because this is one of those rare things – an art form that that is accessible to all. Anyone can create something beautiful and individual with ease, using glass or ceramic tiles in rich and opulent colors. These have an intrinsic beauty and can be placed in infinite and unique combinations according to each individual artist.

Because every mosaic is unique, it is very difficult to say what makes one successful and another less so. There are rules to follow, which helps, and a long tradition of images and techniques to draw on.

The basics of mosaic are not difficult to master but it is a time-consuming process and can be expensive. When starting out it is important to know some of this technical information in order to avoid mistakes and disappointment. A great advantage of mosaic is that it can be as easy as you want it to be; there is no need to start by making a mural that covers a wall and involves plasterers and a vast number of expensive tiles. A beautiful piece of work can be made directly onto a small piece of wood with a basic craft glue, using found objects or broken house tiles. Help can also be found locally from builders and DIY stores as well as from craft shops and books.

One of the joys of mosaic lies in the chance to experiment. Traditional Italian and French tiles are still my favorite but I like to incorporate found objects too – from glass nuggets and beads to photos and buttons. I have also enjoyed making my own tiles from glass and ceramic. When designing a mosaic it is a good idea to have a drawing to work from to plan the colors and movement of the tiles (*andamenti*) but this also provides a good foundation from which to try out new things.

As mosaic increases in popularity, traditional tesserae are easier to source and buy in shops or by mail order. There are now many courses and workshops which can be found through national mosaic societies, libraries, or art schools. Mosaic is largely a solitary occupation and so attending one of these offers a great opportunity to meet people who are interested in the same thing and to discuss ideas or swap information.

In putting together this book I have described a variety of techniques and projects. By following these projects you will discover the ways of working that you prefer. Once you have these under your belt, it will be easy to design your own pieces when you want to, with the confidence to create objects that appeal to you. When I started making mosaics I loved the materials and the finished objects but felt that some of the techniques, such as casting a slab, would be beyond me. Once I discovered how easy these were, however, my confidence grew and I was soon willing to try any technique.

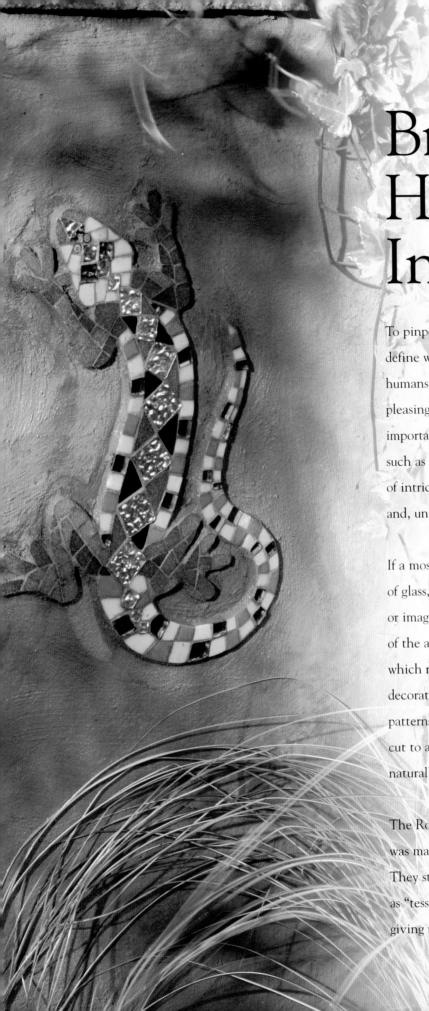

Brief Historical Introduction

To pinpoint the beginning of mosaic you would have to define what is meant by the term. Throughout history humans have arranged pebbles and attractive objects in pleasing patterns and used them to adorn places or objects of importance, either cultural or spiritual. In native cultures, such as aboriginal and Native American, there are examples of intricate pebble and sand patterns, which were ephemeral and, unlike modern mosaic, had no practical function.

If a mosaic is a piece of work, made up of individual tesserae of glass, stone, or ceramic, which forms a permanent pattern or image, then the earliest examples would arguably be those of the ancient Greeks. They created solid floors of pebbles which remain today, and which show that, despite needing no decoration in order to function, they were worked with patterns and images. Over time the stones and pebbles were cut to allow for more detail and intricacy and this led naturally to the use of marble which we still use today.

The Romans style of mosaic is more recognizable today, and was made by using cut stone and glass on floors and walls. They started to cut these materials into what are now known as "tesserae" – cubes that would fit together more closely, giving more control over the image. This was very expensive,

however, and the remaining examples are found in large houses owned by wealthy people. The art of mosaic using tesserae became more widely available to the general public in Italy at this time, where it was made without the expensive colors, and fine examples of monochromatic public pieces can still be seen today. Mosaics spread throughout the Mediterranean and Europe with the expansion of the Roman Empire. They acquired the characteristics of the culture into which they spread while retaining a basic Roman look.

The rise of Christianity brought about the use of glass "smalti" in religious buildings, with the mosaics in Ravenna, Italy being among the best examples. The cathedrals and churches of Europe contain many wonderful examples for both inspiration and education.

Mosaic went into decline following the Renaissance and existed largely as a means of making fine reproductions of paintings – a practice that continued until the Victorian times, when a disposable income and the building of empires caused people to look back in time for inspiration on how to demonstrate their wealth. This was aided by the industrialization of tile production in Venice, which enabled the reverse method to be used. Large areas of mosaic could now be made in the factory and exported all over the globe.

Mosaic continued in this manner until it emerged as a new and exiting art form during the Art Nouveau period – a time which saw the mosaics of Antonio Gaudi and his partner Josep Maria Jujol in Spain covering vast surfaces of buildings with glazed tiles and "found objects." The mosaics of this time show a resurgence of energy and inventiveness, and this artistic interest mosaic was also investigated by artists such as Pablo Picasso, Marc Chagall, and Gustav Klimt.

Following a brief lull in creativity, where mosaic was used largely to "clad" public buildings, today mosaics are made in many contexts, as fine art, to enhance domestic and retail areas, and, increasingly, as community projects. Once more in history people are intrigued by this art form and want to explore its potential while drawing on its traditions and cultural variations. Through modern-day technology, a mosaic artist has access to images of work, and ideas from anywhere in the world. We can "chat" on the Internet to artists working in other countries, purchase materials by mail order, and read books and magazines on the subject. This is a very exiting time to be working with mosaic.

Techniques and Equipment

Planning and Design

Choosing the design that you want is really a matter of personal taste, combined with the practicalities of mosaic technique. For example, a design that is made up predominantly of lines is more difficult to render in mosaic than in drawing or needlework. An image that concentrates on shapes and areas of color, however, work with the material rather than against it.

A mosaic is already made up of hundreds of small parts and therefore the design should be kept as simple as possible. Contrast in color and tone helps, and it is easier to work from a drawing so that potential problems can be ironed out at an early stage. A good general rule is to make a contrast between the image and the background both in color and movement (see *andamenti*, page 24). The Flying Bird Wall Plaque (page 72) uses a very limited palette to good effect because there is no real variety in the size or shape of the tiles. In the Butterfly Table (page 57), the central image is complex in both shape and color and so the surround has been kept monochromatic with regular size and shape pieces to contrast. To help define the central image, an outer line has been stuck around the butterfly to separate it from the background this is called *opus vermiculatum* (see page 24).

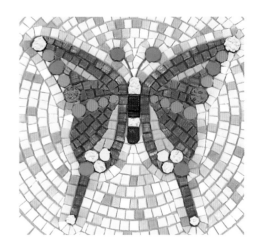

Choosing Tiles

There are no rules about what you can use in a mosaic, which is both liberating and confusing. To start off with, it is easiest to concentrate on traditional tiles (tesserae) because they have an inherent beauty that will ensure success for your mosaic. Also, there is a wealth of information on how to use them.

Tiles can be bought on three different backings, brown paper, mesh, and silicone-bonded. All will come off with soaking although the silicone-bonded ones need longer soaking with hot water and some "gentle" persuasion.

Vitreous glass tiles.

VITREOUS TESSERAE

These are square glass tiles that come on sheets of brown paper and which have to be soaked off before use. They have a flat top to them and a grooved underside, which helps them to adhere to a surface. These are very beautiful, come in a wide range of colors, and are frost-proof. They can be bought in mixed bags, priced by weight, and some craft shops sell them in a pick-and-mix box. Because the colors of the tiles are mixed by eye, there is sometimes a slight discrepancy in the hue. If making a large area of one color, therefore, be sure that you have enough to begin with. Vitreous tiles are now available in different sizes although the 0.8 inch square is still the most common.

SMALTI

This is handmade opaque glass with a brilliant surface. It is made in discs that are then cut by hand. There are different sizes of smalti but the most common is 0.4 x 0.6 inch and it can be bought in mixed bags or by color. Unlike vitreous glass it does not come on sheets and what may appear to be imperfection, such as bubbles and irregular shapes and surfaces, are part of its charm.

GOLD AND SILVER SMALTI

This is handmade by sandwiching a thin layer of gold or silver between two layers of glass which is then cut to size by hand. They are slightly thicker than tesserae, have two smooth surfaces, and are expensive.

Smalti.

MIRROR TILES

These can be bought from tile shops on a canvas backing, and as Indian tiles in various shapes from a mosaic supplier. The Indian tiles are hand cut, are often irregular in shape, and sometimes the silvering is poor but, for some projects, they compliment the "hand-crafted" feel of a mosaic better than factory cut tiles. When applying mirror tiles you must check the manufacturer's instructions since some glues can damage the silvering.

Ceramic tiles.

CERAMIC TILES

These also come in a wide range of colors and can be either glazed or unglazed. The unglazed porcelain tiles have a uniform color through them whereas the glazed ones are bright and shiny. The glaze can be worn or chipped off, however, to reveal the base color.

Both of the above are frost-proof, while glazed earthenware tiles are not. The latter are therefore appropriate for interior jobs only. Some of them are frost-proof but this must be checked before starting on an external job. They are the cheapest mosaic tiles available and therefore very useful for large projects.

Tiles from a tile shop can be cut with nippers or a tile cutter to provide colors and textures that you cannot get from traditional tesserae.

MARBLE TILES

These can be bought polished or tumbled. The latter gives them an aged appearance. Marble can be bought in rods and will need to be cut using a hammer and hardie which is not covered in this book.

Broken house tiles.

BROKEN CHINA

This is a lovely way of using favorite pieces of domestic china that have been broken and is like a patchwork quilt that utilizes old scraps of family material and therefore holds its own history.

FOUND OBJECTS

I like to use a variety of objects in my work in addition to the more traditional materials. For example, I like to use the glass nuggets and shapes that are sold for flower arrangers. I have used pebbles and buttons (with the hook for the cotton cut off using a saw), and I often spend hours in bead shops looking for something that catches my attention (buying beads in bulk by mail order brings the price down enormously). There are no hard-and-fast rules about what can be used and what constitutes a mosaic, so experimenting is fun.

HOMEMADE TILES

Glass tiles such as those used for the Mirror (page 64) can be made from normal glass, which is then cut into the shapes and sizes that you want and decorated. Glass paints are very versatile but need to be used on the reverse of the tile and then backed with something like a foil. This gives a 3-D effect that glows. Tiles can also be made out of clay or porcelain, which involves the use of a kiln and glazes.

Glass shapes.

Choosing Surfaces

PLYWOOD
This is a good surface for interior work, since it is strong and lightweight. Marine ply can be used for external projects but even this can suffer from the wet if it has been attached with non-water-resistant fittings, and all the surfaces have not been sealed.

FIBERBOARD
This is very popular because it is cheap and strong. It is ideal for small projects, such as wall panels and trivets, but I don't use it for larger projects or external work because of warping.

PERSPEX AND GLASS
These have various uses because of their rigidity and are the only transparent surfaces. They enable you to utilize different materials such as transparent tiles and glass objects.

MESH
Sticking the tiles directly onto a plastic mesh enables work to be done directly in the comfort of the studio and at your own speed. It is then transferred to it's final position and embedded in an adhesive before being grouted

CEMENT BACKER BOARD
This surface is an excellent choice for external work because it consists of a cement panel reinforced with plastic mesh and covered with a slim layer of cement. It is weather resistant and will not warp, but it can be heavy for large projects and is expensive and tricky to get hold of. (Cement backer board is not used in this book.)

TILE BACKING BOARD
This is a relatively new product that is very useful. It is a waterproof, lightweight board that will not warp and so external projects can be completed off site and then installed. (Tile backing board is not used in this book.)

Essential basic tool for cutting tesserae.

Glass Paints for the hand made tiles in the mirror project.

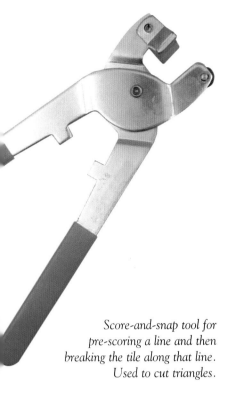

Choosing Adhesives

The practicalities of which adhesive to use for mosaic concerns a lot of people but it is not as complicated as it seems. Every mosaic artist will have their favorite glue, and they may not always agree with each other, so experimentation is important.

WHITE CRAFT GLUE

This comes in two forms, water-soluble (PVA) and non-water-soluble (EVA). Water-soluble glue is diluted 50:50 with water and used to stick down tiles onto brown paper for the reverse method. Non-water-soluble is used for all internal work, for example, panels.

There are also permanent craft glues that can be used for outdoor work, but the correct surface should be used to ensure that the piece is waterproof (see above). These glues can also be added to cement for external work, although most ready-mixed cements have an adhesive mix already included (see cement-based adhesive, below).

SILICONE

This is good to use with glass and perspex because of it's transparency. It is also useful for gluing mirror tiles because it does not damage the silvering on the back.

Score-and-snap tool for pre-scoring a line and then breaking the tile along that line. Used to cut triangles.

EPOXY RESIN

This is a two part glue that is suitable for outdoor use, which is made up of the resin itself and the hardener. They have to be mixed together before use and can be bought from any hardware store in either tube or syringe form. It has a quick drying time and so you have to work on small areas at a time in a well-ventilated room.

CEMENT-BASED ADHESIVE

This is used in many ways and forms in this book. I use a ready-mixed brand to fix the Wall Lizard (page 90) directly on mesh, and a different brand to stick the tiles for the Flying Bird Wall Plaque (page 72) and for the Birdbath (page 95). Using cement often alarms people as it appears to be leaving the world of art and craft and venturing into the world of building. If fact cement is simply a glue that is useful for some projects.

Everyone mixes cement slightly differently, but a good basic rule is three parts sand to one part cement. The raw materials are easy to get at any hardware store, but it is important to include EVA if the mosaic is for external use because this will help the adhesion. (An adhesive mix is included in most ready-made brands, but check on the packaging).

I normally use ready-mix cement adhesive from a DIY store. This is convenient and less messy, which can be very useful, but it is more expensive and this could become an issue for larger pieces. If making your own from scratch, a slurry of dilute cement mixture should be added to the dampened wall or floor before the mosaic is placed. This is only relevant if the mosaic is going on to this sort of surface.

When using the reverse method, the cement is applied to a wall with a notched trowel and then the mosaic is pushed into it.

Cement can also be fun to use in a quick way, applying it to the surface and then pushing tiles and objects into it rapidly in a looser, more informal way.

It is important to remember that cement will only stick to wood if an EVA is added.

Enlarging and Tracing Down

An image can be enlarged by several methods, such as gridding it up and transferring the image to a larger grid but I always use a photocopier for speed and efficiency. It also allows for a bit more flexibility because it is very difficult to change your mind about the size of an image after you have just spent an hour gridding it up.

I use trace down paper for transferring images onto my chosen surface because, unlike carbon paper, which is also good, trace down paper does not have a waxy surface and so it takes the permanent marker better. It is available in several colors.

USING TRACE DOWN PAPER

Secure the drawing to the wood on one side with sticky tape. Sandwich the trace down paper between the wood and the design, chalk-side down. Trace over the image with a sharp pencil or ballpoint pen. When complete, remove all the paper and ink in the image with the permanent marker.

Equipment for drawing out the designs, applying the glue and cutting to fit

Glass cutter for cutting glass squares to make tiles.

Cutting

Mosaics can be made without any cutting, such as the Trivet (page 30) or the Checkerboard (page 33), but to create individual and complex designs, a degree of cutting is necessary. This requires specialist tools called nippers which will cut glass or ceramic tiles. These can be bought from craft shops or DIY tile stores and come in various designs. They must have tungsten tips, a spring, and long "arms." Holding them near the end of the arms enables you to cut hard surfaces with the spring taking the strain. Like most tools nippers do eventually get blunt but can be sharpened by some tool shops or replaced. The metal holders for the spring stop the tungsten tips of the nippers meeting and therefore prevent this happening for a long time.

CUTTING HALVES AND QUARTERS

To start off, ceramic tiles are easiest to cut although the techniques are the same for glass. Holding the nippers firmly in one hand, place the tile just inside the tungsten tips of the nippers at 90 degrees. Hold the tile firmly with the other hand opposite the blades. Press the arms of the nippers closed while exerting the same pressure on the tile between your fingers. The tile will snap along the pressure line into two halves. To create the standard quarter tile most commonly used in mosaic, repeat this action on the half tile, cutting it across the middle.

CIRCLES AND LEAVES

Using a whole tile, draw a circle onto the ceramic tile and hold firmly in one hand. Cut off all four corners and then "nibble" the edges smooth until the circle is achieved. Even though the final shape is a circle, all the cuts are straight and need to be very small. This is definitely a case of less is more – there is no way of replacing a piece cut in error so don't attempt to take away too much each time. As with all cutting, it will take some practice but it is not difficult. Leaves are cut in much the same way, except that only two corners are removed before the tile is nibbled into shape.

 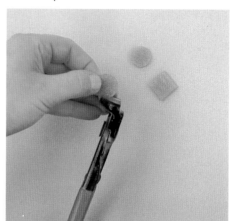

TRIANGLES

These can be cut with normal nippers by placing the tile into the blades at the corner. Only one triangle per tile will be usable and will still need some nibbling. Alternatively, you can use a different tool, which scores the glass and then snaps it. By scoring a line firmly along the diagonal of the tile, the tool can snap it cleanly and you will have two workable triangles from each whole tile.

 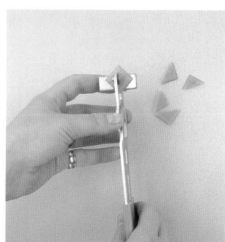

Applying the adhesive

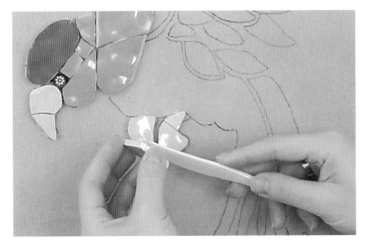

Applying adhesive with a brush.

Applying adhesive with a knife.

When using wood bases for the work, it is useful to score the surface with a sharp knife to create more texture for the glue to stick to.

Having done this there are two main ways to apply the glue in the direct method, either onto the surface or onto the tile. To begin with it is much easier to glue or "butter" each tile individually as this gives more control and thinking time. Once you have more experience, it is possible to lay a line of glue directly onto the surface and then place the tiles onto them. I still prefer the "buttering" technique as long as there is no deadline, because I enjoy the process and have no wish to hurry it.

The glue in the direct method is actually mainly for anchoring the tiles until they are grouted and therefore it is important not to use too much glue for the grout to work. Another problem of too much glue is that, if it squeezes up between the tiles, it can show up in the grout, destroying the look of the piece.

Always read the manufacturer's instructions before starting a piece and, if in doubt, ask at the store where you bought it. Some glues, such as epoxy resin, can dry in minutes whereas a water-based PVA for the indirect method on paper stays malleable for a long time and, even when it dries, the tile can be soaked off. Always read the safety instructions before using.

Direct and Indirect/Reverse Methods

There are two basic methods of making a mosaic, the direct and the indirect (reverse) methods. They each have their special uses and it is important to choose the correct one for the job in hand.

THE DIRECT METHOD

In this method the tiles are glued directly onto the prepared surface, face up, so that the final image is immediately visible. This is the easiest method to start with and the one that allows you to have more control over the image and its detail, while allowing scope for spontaneity. Each tile is placed individually using a bed of adhesive. The resulting surface is slightly uneven, therefore, and the tiles reflect the light differently. This effect can be used to achieve a glittering surface and is suitable for decorative areas that do not need to be flat, for example wall panels, bowls, and 3-D objects. It is also the best method to use with found objects of an irregular shape and depth.

THE INDIRECT/REVERSE METHOD

In this method the tiles are temporarily stuck upside down onto a surface like strong brown paper using a water based glue. Leave at least 0.04 inch between the pieces because the paper will absorb water from the glue and it will expand slightly. When it dries it contracts again and the tiles are pulled closer together. If they have been stuck too closely together they may become unstuck or will not lie flat again. Working on paper stretched on a board can prevent this problem. When the design is complete, the mosaic is embedded in a prepared surface such as tile adhesive and the paper is removed by soaking once the adhesive is dry. This method is ideal for surfaces that need to be flat, such as a floor or table top. The final result can lack the exciting surface of a direct piece of work, but will have a calm feeling of regularity. If the surface is even and flat, it is easier to concentrate on the colors and detail.

Casting

Casting a mosaic in a concrete slab is a very satisfying way of working and is used to create a strong flat surface using the reverse method. The final result has a solidity and durability that is very attractive. Mosaic has historically always been used for flooring and this is a safe and practical way of making either one stone slab for decoration, or stepping stones, or joining the two together to create a larger area.

By casting a piece of mosaic, it is possible to use irregular sizes and shapes while ensuring that there is one flat surface to be walked on; any pieces that protrude when stuck on the paper will become submerged in the concrete once the paper has been turned upside down, leaving an even surface.

Float for smoothing the cement in the slab.

Trowel for mixing the cement and putting it into the frame.

Slab-casting frame.

Grouting

Grouting is an integral part of the mosaic technique. It is not merely filling in the gaps or securing the tiles in place but part of the design. Until the mosaic is grouted it has the purity of color that you see in pointillist paintings or tapestry stitches but, once grouted, the nature of it changes. There are therefore two areas to look at: the technical side of which materials to use; and the creative one of how to choose the color, pattern, and size of the grouted areas. (see *andamenti*, page 25)

Grouting Squeegee for pressing the grout into the gaps between the tiles.

In choosing the correct grout to use, there are some things to consider. Firstly whether to use a proprietary brand either in powder form or ready mixed, or whether to mix it using sand and cement in the traditional way. There are now so many good grouts available in the shops that I always buy mine. I usually buy it in powder form and add water so that it is the consistency that I need. It is important to check on the packet, however, to see what size space the grout is to fill so that it is compatible. If you choose a grout for a small gap and then use it in a large one it will crack once dry. There is little choice of colors available but it is easy to dye the grout using commercial cement dyes available from builders' merchants.

The color of the grout is important because of its effect on the colored tiles around it. The design may call for a contrasting color so that a dark blue sky has light gray grout to show the pattern and movement of the tiles, or it might need a dark grout so that there is no distraction from the overall color. A grout can subdue or enhance the colors around it, and therefore should be chosen as carefully as the colors of the tiles themselves. As a basic rule it is a good idea to avoid white, since it is very difficult to use this well; it can dominate the image and flatten all the colors. Always ensure that you make up enough grout at the beginning of the job so that you do not have to mix some more mid-project. This is especially important when making a colored grout because of the difficulties of matching the color.

There are some occasions when it is not necessary to grout a piece of mosaic, for example when using smalti (which is not used in this book), because of all the natural holes and bubbles that would hold the grout and look unsightly. For a majority of mosaics, however, the grouting is an integral part of the whole.

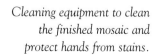

Cleaning equipment to clean the finished mosaic and protect hands from stains.

1. Mix the powdered grout to a firm consistency (see packet instructions).

2. Spread the grout evenly onto the tiles.

3. Using a squeegee, press the grout into all of the spaces.

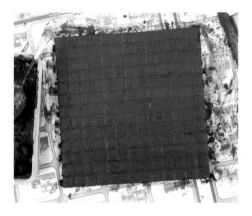

4. Continue until the entire surface is covered.

5. Using a clean cloth remove the surface grout.

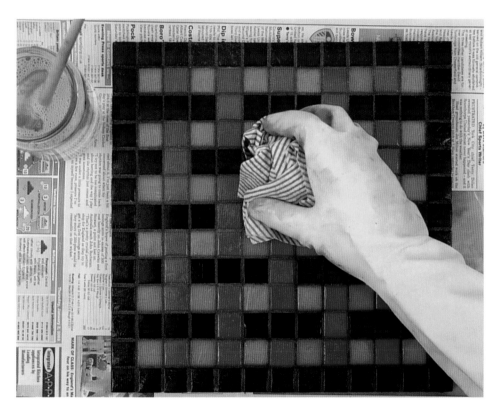

6 Remove excess grout using an acid-based tile cleaner.

Once dry, buff the surface with a soft cloth.

PRE-GROUTING

When the reverse method is used the finished mosaic can be pre-grouted before it is embedded in the adhesive. This is done so that the grout goes into all of the spaces behind the tiles and ensures that there are no air pockets to weaken the piece and allow frost and moisture to damage it. Pre-grouting is an industry standard for the building trade, but is not always done in mosaics for the home. It is particularly advisable when the mosaic is for external use.

Andamenti

This is the term used for the direction of the tiles in a mosaic made by the grout lines or interstices (the gaps between the tiles) before they are grouted. It is often referred to as the "coursing," and is essential to give form and clarity to the piece. When planning a mosaic it is important to give this as much consideration as you give the tiles themselves and, in projects such as the birdbath, I have drawn the flow of tiles onto the bath with chalk so that I can rub it out and redo it until I am satisfied.

There are many different *andamenti* techniques to use many of which have their own names starting with the Latin word *opus* which means work

OPUS VERMICULATUM

This is a line of tesserae formed around the central image to emphasize it (see Butterfly Table, page 57). This line can be repeated out to fill a larger space, creating movement and rhythm, or it can isolate the image and create a barrier between the image and a contrasting flow of tiles (see opposite).

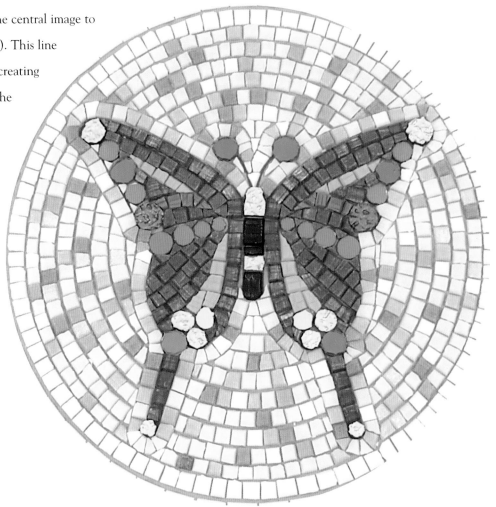

OPUS REGULATUM

In this method the tiles are laid in straight lines which form a grid. When you buy a sheet of tiles they are a perfect example of this but, when making a mosaic, it is very difficult to achieve such symmetry. They can also be laid offset as in brickwork so that they only match in one direction and is then known as *opus tessalatum*. This is one of the two main ways of laying tiles for large areas and backgrounds along with *opus palladianum* (see below).

OPUS PALLADIANUM

This method resembles a crazy paving path because the tiles are cut randomly and the only consistent factor is the width of the grout (see Snail Slab, page101, or Elephant, page 106). This is an easy method for a beginner because there are no rules for the size or shape of the pieces and so it is quick and easy.

Cleaning and Finishing Off

Once a mosaic has been grouted it may look clean but there is one last stage to do. However hard you have worked to clean the grout off there will inevitably be some left, and this can be removed with a good-quality tile cleaner from a DIY store or builders' merchants. These products contain an acid which cleans off excess grout. I wear rubber gloves for safety and, using an old toothbrush or paintbrush dipped in the cleaner, I apply it liberally to the finished and grouted piece of work. The acid will make the excess grout on the tiles fizz. Once the cleaner is rinsed off the mosaic is clean and free of dirt. The cleaner must be rinsed off well or the acid will continue to eat into the grout. Try the cleaner out on sparse tiles first and if using found objects, keep some aside to test.

When the mosaic is clean there are also products to prevent staining and dirt. Again this must be done with advice because it is possible to get the wrong product, which will not soak into the tiles but will remain as a covering that can damage the tiles and attract dirt.

Once the piece is dry, buff the work with a dry duster or cloth or, in the case of a large piece of work, a masonry brush can be used. This will not work in the case of unglazed ceramic tiles and so the last clean after grouting will be the final chance to remove all the marks.

Priming the edges.

Glossing the edges to finish the off the piece.

Safety

- Wear gloves when handling cement-based substances.

- Wear goggles if there is a danger of flying glass.

- Wear a nose and mouth mask when cutting tiles, especially house tiles, and always when mixing cement and grout.

- Work in a well-ventilated room when cutting or using glue.

- Always clear surfaces with a brush – never your hand.

- Keep children and animals out of the room where you are working.

- Don't dispose of substances such as grout and cement down the sink because it may set and cause blockages.

- Keep food and drink away from the area where you are cutting tiles.

First Time Mosaics

This section contains simple, first-time projects for people who want to try their hand at mosaics but who have no experience. The first three projects in this section use uncut tiles of different sizes and shapes so you can get used to handling the materials without concerns about shaping the tiles or the expense of wastage.

Trivet *Direct method*

A mosaic trivet for the center of a table is both decorative and functional. It is a good project to start on because of its simple shape and, if the size is planned carefully to accommodate the tiles, there is no need for cutting. This allows the freedom to play with color and pattern, and it is very easy to progress to a design of your own. I have used glass tiles because of their beauty and because, unlike some ceramic tiles, they do not stain and are heat resistant.

MATERIALS

Vitreous tiles – see color palette

Fiberboard (MDF) or plywood 11 x 11 inches

White paper for design

Pencil

Trace down paper

Permanent marker

Sharp knife

White craft glue (EVA) and brush

Rubber groves

Grout and squeegee

Clean cloth

Tile cleaner

Black namel or gloss paint, primer, brush, and cleaner.

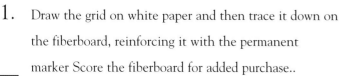

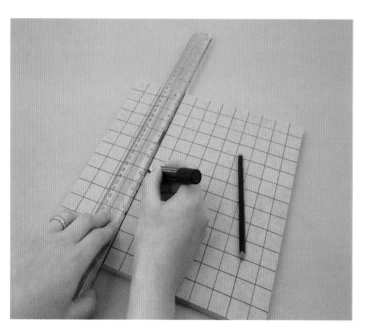

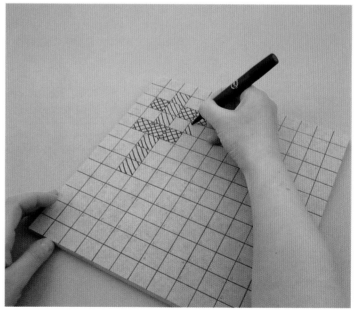

1. Draw the grid on white paper and then trace it down on the fiberboard, reinforcing it with the permanent marker Score the fiberboard for added purchase..

2. By crosshatching the pattern in at this stage there is less chance of becoming confused and putting the wrong color tiles down later.

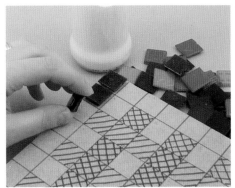
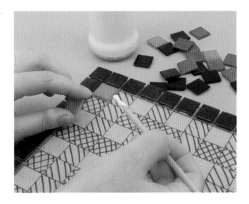

3. Starting with the dark red tiles for the border, use the brush to apply glue to the reverse (grooved) side of the tiles. Do not put it on too thickly or it will ooze out between the tiles, but make sure there is enough to cover the back. Continue until the border is complete.

4. Begin the central pattern by sticking down the first color using the crosshatching on the board to ensure that the pattern is correct.

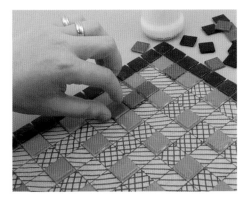

5. Continue the design by adding the second color tiles.

6. Glue the third color tiles in place to complete the pattern.

7. Leave 24 hours for the glue to dry thoroughly. Be careful at this stage because, until the work is grouted, the tiles are vulnerable to damage. Grout and clean the mosaic and paint the edges following the instructions on page 21–26.

Checkerboard

Direct method

Chess sets have an intrinsic beauty that is rarely matched by the board, and which is usually a piece of folded paper or board that is put away when the game has finished. By making a permanent checkerboard you can create an object that will always encourage people to play, can be left out set up as part of the furniture, and which will last as long as the pieces themselves. I have chosen a glass chess set to complement the glass tiles.

MATERIALS

Vitreous tiles in two sizes (see color palette)

Fiberboard (MDF) or plywood 21.25 x 21.25 inches

White paper for the design

Pencil

Trace down paper

Permanent marker

Sharp knife

White craft glue (EVA) and brush

Rubber gloves

Grout and squeegee

Clean cloth

Tile cleaner

Black enamel or gloss paint, primer, brush, and brush cleaner

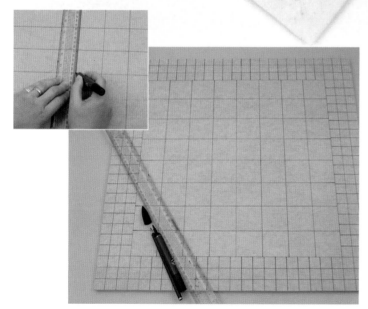

1. Transfer the design from white paper to the fiberboard using the trace down paper, and reinforce with a permanent marker. Score the board for added purchase.

2. Crosshatch the squares for the border to clarify which colors are used where in the pattern.

3. Starting with the large black and white tiles, glue each tile down.

4. Be careful to keep the space between the tiles even.

5. Start on the first color for the border, laying the tiles out carefully according to the design.

6. Continue the design by adding the second color tiles.

7. Glue the third color tiles in place to complete the pattern.

8. Leave 24 hours for the glue to dry thoroughly. Be careful at this stage because, until the tiles are grouted, they are vulnerable to being chipped or dislodged. Grout and clean the mosaic and paint the edges of the board following the instructions on pages 21–26.

Sun Catcher *Direct method ungrouted*

Mosaic has a long history and has developed over the years as new materials have been invented and discovered. The use of silicone glue enables us to stick clear glass tiles and other objects to clear glass or perspex. While this isn't a traditional mosaic method, it enables us to get the full glory of the glass in a way that wasn't available before. Glass is such a beautiful material that it seems a pity to leave this aspect of it to the stained glass artists and therefore I have included this project .

MATERIALS
Collection of transparent glass tiles and
glass beads (see color palette)
Perspex 7.75 x 13 inches, with holes drilled
White paper for the design
Pencil
Silicone glue
Sharp knife
Wire for hanging

I have used flower arrangers' beads and shapes that combine well with the transparent tiles to create the design. While feeling at liberty to use anything transparent that has caught my eye, I have retained the feel of a mosaic in t formality of my design and the use of repeated squares.

1. Draw the design out onto a piece of white paper the same size as the perspex.

2. Place the perspex on top of the design with the holes at the top and start to stick down the tiles, beginning with the border and being careful not to cover the drilled holes. Do not add too much glue because it is difficult to remove later if it oozes out onto the perspex. (Excess glue can be cut off when dry with a sharp knife.)

3. Keep the design very even and, when putting in the glass beads or other objects, place the tiles around them first – to keep the spacing correct – before gluing the irregular shapes.

4. There is no grouting, but regular spacing will provide continuity amid the mixture
    of colors and shapes.

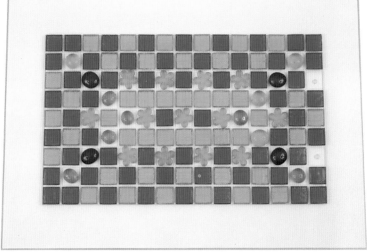

5. Continue gluing the tiles until you reach a single line in
    the middle.

6. The glue takes 12 hours to dry completely, although it is
    touch-dry in 15 minutes. There is no need to grout or
    clean this piece so when it is dry, thread the wire through
    the holes ready to hang.

Picture Frame *Direct method*

This mosaic has a function to fulfill, it must complement the picture or photograph and not distract from it, while being attractive in its own right.

This design uses ceramic tiles in a muted range of colors to create a subtle border with a minimum of cutting. Ceramic tiles are easier to cut than glass ones and therefore this is an easy project for a beginner.

MATERIALS

Ceramic tiles (see color palette)

Millefiori, beads, or vitreous tiles

Picture frame 10.8 x 12.8 inches

(Frame width 2 inches)

White paper for the design

Pencil

Trace down paper

Permanent marker

Sharp knife

Nippers

White craft glue (EVA) and brush

Rubber gloves

Grout and squeegee

Clean cloth

Tile cleaner

Glass to fit finished frame

1. First draw the design on white paper, then trace it onto the picture frame and reinforce with a permanent marker. Score the wood for better adhesion.

2. Begin by cutting the black and white tiles for the border (see page 16) and sticking them down.

3. Cut and stick the inner border tiles. (Check that you have left sufficient room between them for the whole tiles.)

4. Stick the whole white tiles down

5. Cut the leaves from green tiles by removing the opposite corners (see page 17).

6. Cut the circles for the flowers. I have used millefiori for the centers but a small circle of vitreous glass or a bead will work just as well. When they are cut, glue them into place.

7. Fill the gaps at the top and bottom with two more leaves.

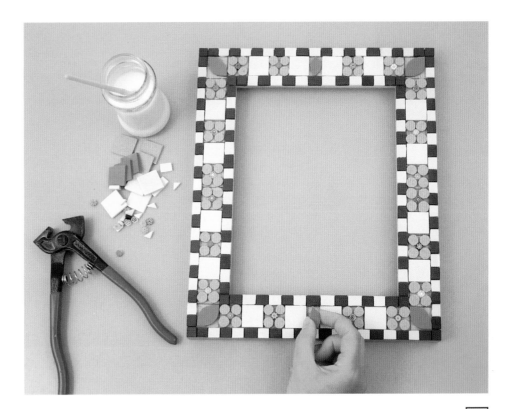

8. Cut small white triangles to complete the corner squares.

9. The finished piece is now ready to grout and clean (see pages 21–26). Reassemble the picture frame with the fitted glass.

Mosaics for Shape and Color

In this section the projects start to use a greater variety of shapes and colors while keeping the designs simple.

House Number Plate *Direct method*

A house number plate has a function that must not be confused by the design; it must be clear and easy to read and therefore the design here has been kept simple both in form and in the color palette. The color range is kept simple so that it can be changed for one that matches your front door or house coloring.

This number plate is for a sheltered porch and therefore I have used EVA but, if there is a greater threat from the weather, epoxy resin can be used.

When putting two numbers next to each other, either leave a gap just big enough for grout or a gap big enough for a quarter tile. A space that is in between the two is very difficult to cut without looking bitty.

MATERIALS

Vitreous tiles (see color palette)

Exterior or marine plywood 9.4 x 8.6 x 0.8 inches

(to allow for one tile depth at the edge)

White paper for the design

Pencil

Trace down paper

Permanent marker

Sharp knife

Drill

Nippers

White craft glue (EVA) and brush

Silicone waterproofer and brush

Rubber gloves

Grout and squeegee

Clean cloth

Two screws, rawl plugs, and screwdriver

Tile cleaner

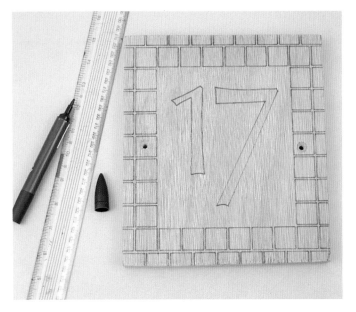

1. Draw the image on white paper and trace it down onto the plywood. Reinforce with a permanent marker and score with a knife. Drill and countersink holes for the screws

2. Cut and stick the quarter tiles for the checkered surround, taking care not to put any tiles over the holes.

3. Cut the blue tiles in half and stick them around the outside of the border pattern. I have left larger grout spaces between these to emphasize the geometric nature and to make the grout part of the design.

4. Cut the yellow tiles for the number and glue into place

5. Fill in the space around the numbers with a single color.

6. Stick the tiles around the edge of the plywood. Tiles on the outer edge of an object can be vulnerable to being knocked, but a house number plate is usually out of range of any danger and therefore is safe.

7. Seal the back of the plywood with the silicone waterproofer and now the number plate is ready to be attached to the wall.

8. Grout the piece avoiding, the screw holes. Drill corresponding holes in the outer wall and fix the number plate in position.

9. Once it is secure, glue the eight final tiles in place, grout, and clean the whole piece following the instructions on pages 21–26.

Fruit Bowl *Direct method*

A fruit bowl tends to be a permanent item on a kitchen table and should be a thing of beauty, reflecting the colors and shapes of the fruit. By making it in mosaic, it is easy to wipe clean and always looks attractive, even when nearly empty. Unlike the table-top project (see page 57), there is no need for the surface to be absolutely even and therefore it is a good project to do in the direct method.

MATERIALS

Vitreous tiles (see color palette)

Clean, dry terra-cotta dish 12.2 inches diameter

White paper for the design

Pencil

Trace down paper

Permanent marker

Nippers

White craft glue (EVA) and brush

Rubber gloves

Grout and squeegee

Terra-cotta cement coloring

Clean cloth

Tile cleaner

1. Draw the design onto white paper and trace it down onto the dish, reinforcing the image with the permanent marker.

2. Cut and stick the dark green tiles to the top of the leaf, keeping a strong line down the middle for the center vein.

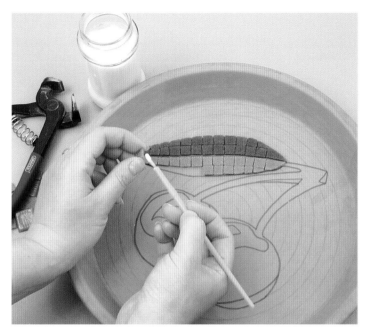

3. There is no grouting to be done at this stage, but regular spacing will provide some continuity amid the mixture of colors and shapes.

4. Starting with the first cherry, cut the white highlight and glue it in place.

5. Cut and glue the red tiles in place, forming lines that accentuate the shape of the cherry. Start with the lightest shade and progress through the darker shades.

6. Finish by cutting the darkest red tiles to shape and glue them down.

7. Repeat with the second cherry.

8. Use a light brown to construct the stalks making them get thinner toward the cherries. Add a small dark brown shadow at the top of the stalks

9. Stick a line of mixed blue tiles around the image (*opus vermiculatum*, page 24).

10. Using the concentric circles as a guide, fill in the background using a random mixture of the blue tiles.

11. When sticking the tiles to the side of the dish it helps to leave them with the glue on them for between 30–45 minutes before sticking them to the dish. This enables the glue to semi-dry stopping the tiles sliding down the sides.

12. The dish is now ready to grout and clean following the instructions on pages 21–26. Adding terra-cotta dye to the mixture will make it look as if the tiles are set into the dish itself and give it a feeling of age and solidity.

Butterfly Table

Indirect method on paper

I like to use the butterfly as an image in mosaic because of the beauty of its colors and pattern; it provides a good example of how the way that the tiles are placed describes the shape and movement of the subject.

NB The table kit I have used is made from interior-quality wood and is therefore not suitable for external use. If you want a table for the garden, you must use cement-based adhesive and a marine/external plywood top with metal legs. For increased protection, you can put a tile backing board on the table top or a sheet of cement board. I have also not pre-grouted this project, unlike the snail slab (see page 101), because it is not for external use and is unlikely to lift.

MATERIALS

Vitreous tiles (see color palette), gold smalti, and mirror tiles

Table kit 15.9 inches diameter

Brown paper and scissors

White paper for the design

Pencil

Trace down paper

Permanent marker

White craft glue (PVA), watered down 50:50 and brush

Nippers

Rapid-setting cement-based adhesive

Notched trowel

Rubber gloves

Grout and squeegee

Sponge

Tile cleaner

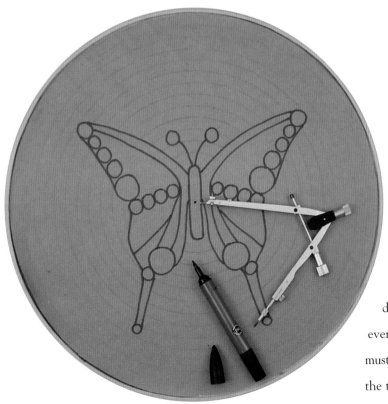

1. First draw the image on white paper. Cut the strong brown paper slightly smaller than the table top. Trace down your image onto the matte side and reinforce the drawing with the permanent marker. (The image will eventually be reversed so if words or numbers are added they must be designed back to front.) Keep the work in progress on the table top to provide a solid surface of the right size.

2. Apply the mosaic tiles upside down (ridged-side up) to the paper using the watered-down craft glue. Make sure that they are not too close together to avoid them touching if the paper shrinks with the glue, which may make the surface uneven. Don't be tempted to use too much glue because the adhesion is only temporary. Symmetry is important in the design; therefore I have started with the body and worked out. (I wanted the blue underside of the ripple gold to show, so the gold surface is face up.)

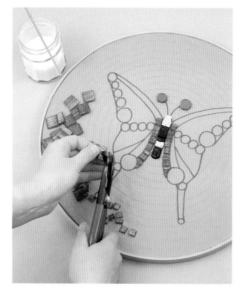

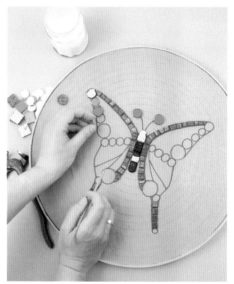

3. Cut the gold tiles into circles for the ends of the antennae, and stick them in place. The thin lines depicting the antennae themselves will be formed by spaces left between the background tiles.

4. Cut and stick the tiles to form the curve of the wings radiating out from the body. By doing both of these at the same time the butterfly will have a balanced appearance.

5. Using a mixture of circles cut from plain gold, ripple gold, and mirror tiles, place the shapes that make up the outside edge of the wings. (Remember to put these tiles upside down, although both sides of the gold tiles can be used to effect in this design).

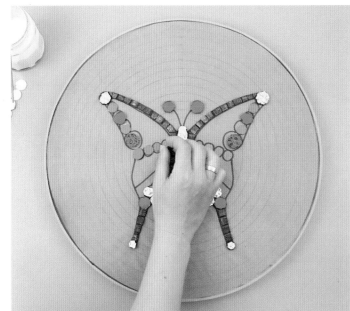 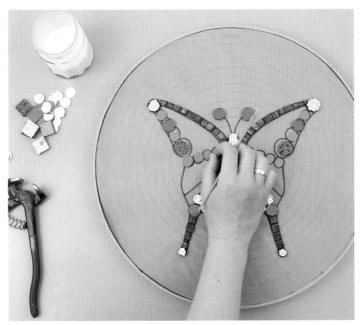

6. Cut and glue mirror circles to divide each wing.

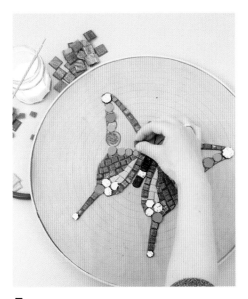 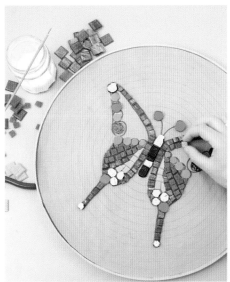 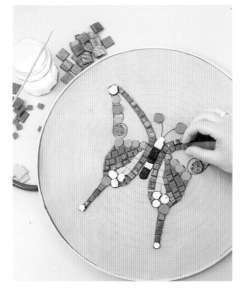

7. Fill in the rest of the wings in lines, showing the movement of the wing.

8. Glue a line of tiles around the image (*opus vermiculatum*, page 24).

9. Proceed to lay the background tiles in concentric circles using the drawn circles as guidelines. Making the last layer pure white helps the definition.

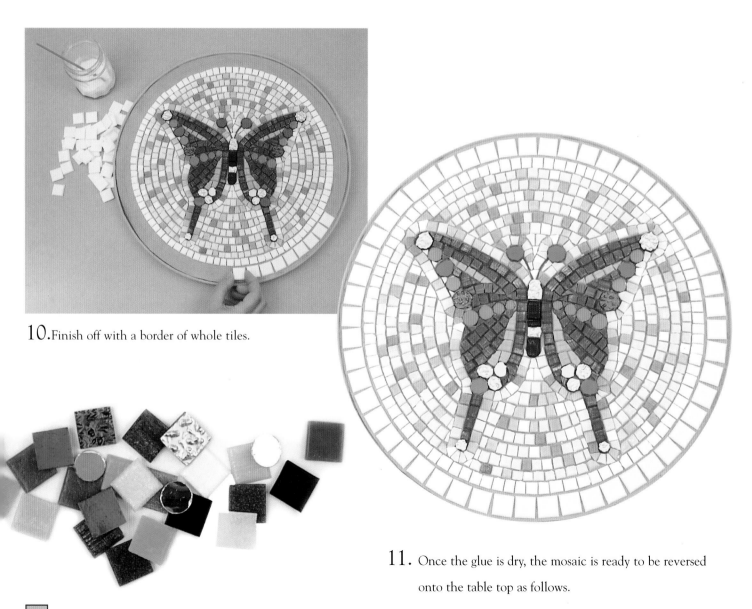

10. Finish off with a border of whole tiles.

11. Once the glue is dry, the mosaic is ready to be reversed onto the table top as follows.

12. Seal the table top with a 50:50 coat of PVA and water and, when it is dry, apply a layer of cement-based adhesive with a 0.1 inch notched trowel, making sure that you press down to the wood to ensure the right amount of adhesive is used.

13. Place the mosaic, paper-side up onto the adhesive. Make sure that you are happy with the placing because it cannot be repositioned without the risk of losing small tiles off the paper. Press gently but firmly to make sure that it has stuck, and tamp down with a piece of wood or level out gently with a rolling pin. Clean excess cement from the surface and edges of the mosaic with a sponge.

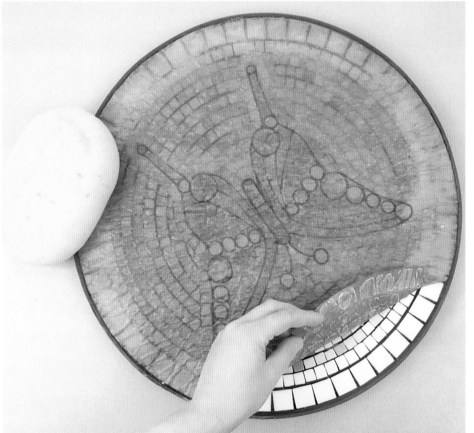

14. Leave until the adhesive is dry and then thoroughly wet the paper with a sponge and leave it to absorb the water for 15–20 minutes.

15. Peel the paper gently back from the edges into the middle. Do not attempt to remove the paper in one go but carefully peel it inward from at least four places. If any tiles come off don't worry, just replace them making sure that there is enough cement adhesive underneath. Clean the mosaic with the wrung out sponge, leave the table top to dry, and grout and clean following the instructions on pages 21–26.

Mirror *Direct method*

This mirror looks opulent and exotic but is very easy to achieve. Most of the tiles have been handmade, which sounds difficult, but they are fun and simple to make. This project is the mosaic equivalent of dress jewelry; it looks good but is affordable and therefore can be more adventurous than a project using expensive gold tiles.

MATERIALS

Plain glass squares 0.8 inch square (these can be cut at a glaziers/framers or at home with a glass cutter); vitreous tiles; mirror tiles

Glass paints, gold outliner, and brushes

White spirit/Mock silver leaf or gold/silver foils as desired

White craft glue (PVA) and brush

Mirror with wooden surround 15 x 15 inches

White paper for the design

Pencil

Trace down paper

Permanent marker

Rubber gloves

Grout and squeegee

Clean cloth

Tile cleaner

Enamel of gloss paint, primer, brush, and cleaner

1. Decide on the color scheme and assemble assorted vitreous, mirror, and glass tiles in your own choice of color. Select some foil backings from craft stores and choose the glass paints.

2. Using the gold outliner, draw any designs onto the glass tiles.

3. Color in the glass tiles with the paints using the gold as outlines. Some can be just painted without any gold lines. Leave them to one side for 24 hours to dry.

4. Meanwhile, coat one side of the glass tiles to be foiled with the craft glue and lay them down carefully onto the assorted foils. Leave 24 hours to dry.

5. Now that the painted tiles are dry, back them with the mock silver leaf by coating the backs with the craft glue and laying them down carefully on the silver. Leave for 24 hours.

6. All of the tiles can be removed or cut off the foils and then they are ready to stick down onto the mirror.

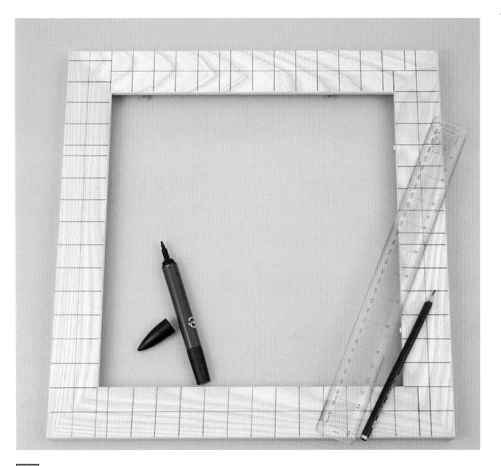

7. Remove the mirror from the frame, if possible, and draw the grid onto the frame, reinforcing the lines with a permanent marker. The grid is not necessary, but can make it easier ensure that the tiles will fit the frame without any odd shapes left over. It is also a good start to give confidence and to create an even pattern which complements the random color and design of the tiles.

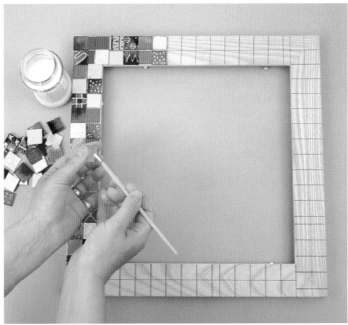

8. The design of the piece is completely up to the individual and so there are no rules. To get the effect that you want it, is often easier to lay the tiles out first and move them around until you achieve a look that you like. Once you have done this glue the tiles down.

9. Leave to dry before grouting.

10. When the glue is dry grout the piece and clean following the instructions on pages 21–26. Prime and paint the edges (both inside and out) of the frame in a color to complement the tiles.

Mosaics with a Difference

The first two projects introduce the use of broken
tiles and found objects while the third simply creates
a repeated image that is in relief.

Flying Bird Wall Plaque

Direct method onto a wall

This method avoids the necessity for transferring the mosaic and fixing it in place once it has been made. It also changes the way you work by forcing you to work standing as if at an easel. This can create an image with more movement and spontaneity, as you stick the pieces of tile as you go without laying them out first.

Using broken house tiles rather than vitreous tiles creates a different look because a simplicity is dictated by the materials. The range of colors is less subtle and it is not possible to cut small and intricate shapes but it is an easier medium for cutting and nibbling large, unusual shapes. The result is an exciting and bright mosaic which is especially useful for larger areas. By keeping the color palette very simple and restricted in this project I have played to its strengths. It is important to work with the materials and not to try and recreate a vitreous mosaic just on a larger scale.

MATERIALS

Broken wall tiles (see color palette)

Clean or freshly rendered area of wall
17.7 x 17.7 inches)

White paper for the design

Pencil

Trace down paper

Permanent marker

Nippers

Quick-drying cement-based adhesive (external
quality for an external piece)

Rubber gloves

Grout and squeegee

Clean cloth

Tile cleaner

1. First draw the design onto white paper and transfer it to the wall using trace down paper. Reinforce the lines with the permanent marker. (If working on a freshly rendered, wet wall, you can "trace" the design by pricking holes through the paper – along the lines of the image – using a sharp implement.

2. Take the whole tiles and roughly break them using a hammer or the tile nippers.

3. Start cutting the pieces of tile for the bird's beak and feet and nibbling them into shape. Stick them down by "buttering" the backs, which will give you more time for this complicated bit.

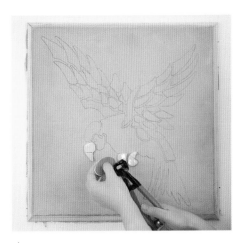

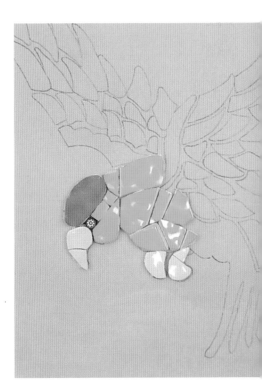

4. Cut the tiles for the head and body and stick them down as you go.

5. Cut the shapes for the front wing. There is no need for slavish accuracy in this method but it is important to keep the feel of the bird by making the shapes sympathetic to the movement. If, when cutting, you achieve a different shape to that drawn out, use it and it will keep the image lively and spontaneous.

6. Once this is finished start on the second wing.

7. Then work down to complete the tail.

8. Cut and stick the blue tiles down to fit around the bird.

9. When the adhesive is dry, grout and clean the mosaic following the instructions on pages 21–26.

Fish Clock *Direct method*

Most rooms in a house have a clock in them and they are mostly very traditional and simple. In this project I have kept the traditional shape and layout, but decorated it to catch the eye. I have done it in the direct method so that the slightly uneven surface will catch the light as it changes through the day.

I love stained glass and wanted to use thick dark lines to separate strong colors with this project. The blues and greens of the sea lend themselves to this and by using the metal fish instead of making mosaic ones, blocks of color can exist alone as if they are a complete piece of glass.

MATERIALS

Metal fish; glass bubbles or circular mirror tiles;

black ceramic tiles; vitreous tiles (see color palette)

Circular clock kit 15.9 inches diameter

White paper for the design

Pencil

Trace down paper

Permanent marker

White craft glue (EVA) and brush

Nippers

Rubber gloves

Grout and squeegee

Clean cloth

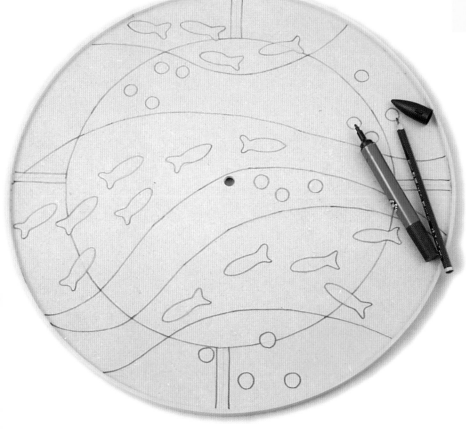

1. First draw the design on white paper, then trace down onto the clock base, reinforcing the image with the permanent marker.

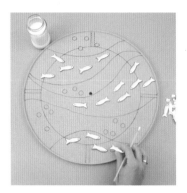
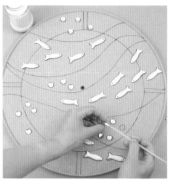

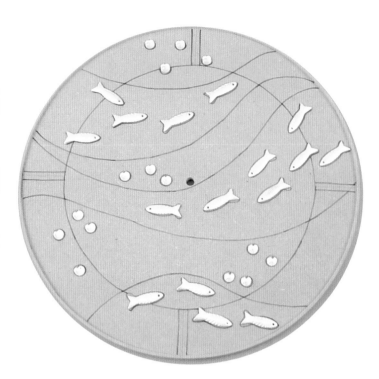

2.   Glue the metal fish and the glass bubbles into position.

3.   Cut the black ceramic tiles into quarters and then cut each quarter again. Using these standard size pieces, stick them in lines where the 12 o'clock, 3 o'clock, 6 o'clock, and 9 o'clock go.

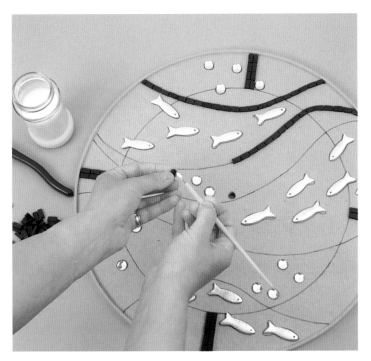
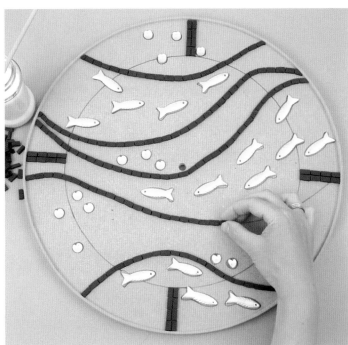

4. Again, using the standard-size black ceramic tiles, stick them along the lines of the water.

5. Organise the colors that you are using so that they are in pairs. Do one complete section across the clock at a time so that the colors don't get confusing. The lighter color will always go in the center of the design and the darker one round the outside. Begin at the bottom of the clock with the first pair.

6. Continue working in pairs of colors up the clock keeping the tiles moving in the same direction as the black guidelines and remembering to separate the inner and outer circles.

7. Make sure not to obstruct the hole that will be needed to fit the clock mechanism in.

8. Continue until all the water is complete.

9. When the clock is complete, allow to
dry, then grout and clean following
the instructions on pages 21–26.
Fix the clock mechanism to the
base.

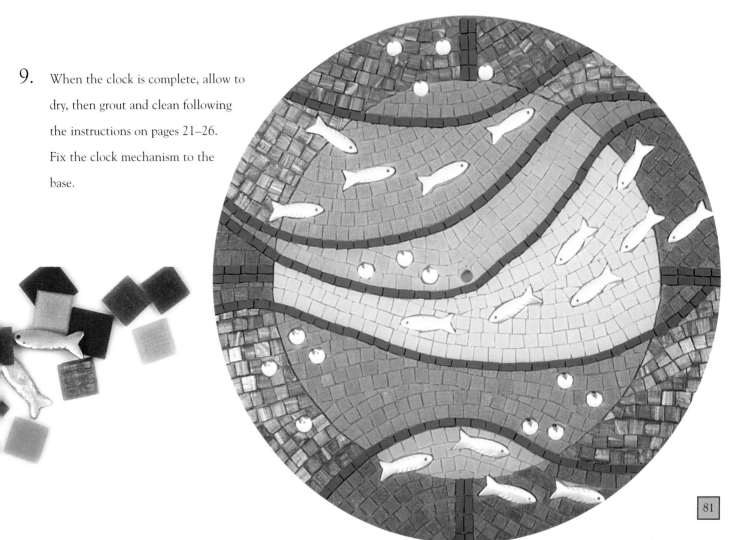

Plant Pot with Ladybugs

Direct method in relief

Decorating a garden pot in this way has no function and therefore there are no restrictions on the shape and image used. I have chosen a ladybug motif for its bright colors and simple shape. The predominant color of red is complementary to green and will show up well against the foliage of the plants. The image is linked to the garden by the subject matter but is stylized and fun.

If the image is enlarged, the black dots may have to be made up of several tiles rather than one. Otherwise, use a large tile as in the checkerboard (page 33).

1. Draw the design on white paper, then trace it out to size on the pot. Sticking onto a curved surface is trickier than on the flat, so choose your pot accordingly. Also, consider the size of the image, it is easier to cut and stick larger pieces of glass so don't be tempted to make the ladybugs too small.

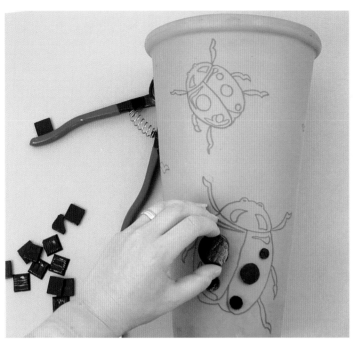

2. If you use a curved pot it is easier to keep it still by resting it on a folded towel. Start by cutting and gluing down the black spots on the first ladybug using the black vitreous tiles. Be careful when placing the tiles not to let them slip because the glue will stain the terra-cotta and not come off.

3. Cut and glue the pink tiles for the highlights.

4. Fill in the wings with the bright red, leaving a straight line down the center of the wings.

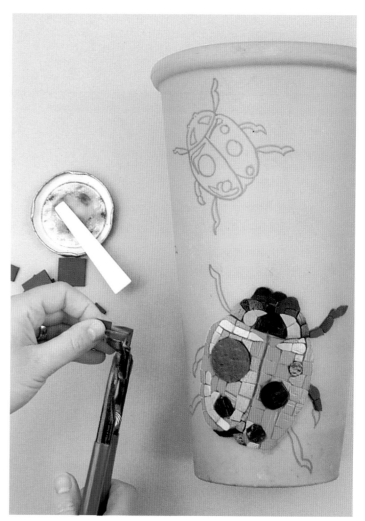

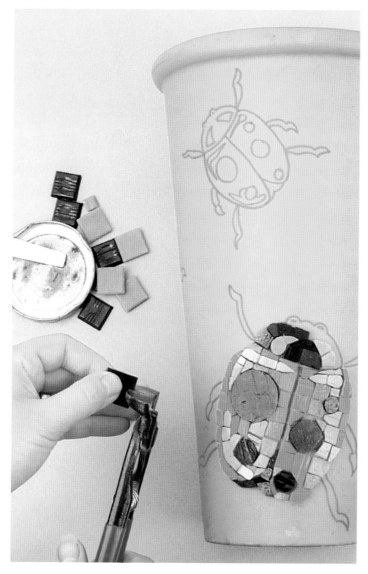

6. Cut the ceramic black tiles to form the legs, and glue so that they touch each other. By using these tiles instead of vitreous tiles you can create a contrast between the shiny wings and the legs, which will help the design to work.

5. Using the vitreous black and gray tesserae, glue down the tiles for under the wings and the head.

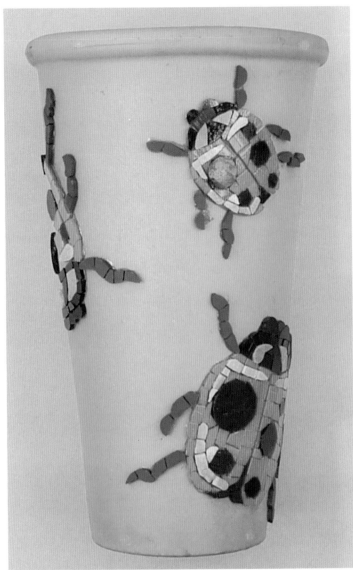

7. Once the first ladybug is finished repeat this for as many ladybugs as you want. The pot is now ready for grouting.

8. Mix some grout with black coloring and grout the ladybugs' bodies. Be careful not to get the grout on the terra-cotta because the black will leave a stain. There is no need to grout the legs; they will look more fragile in contrast to the body. Repeat this process for all the ladybugs and clean each one following the instructions on pages 21–26.

Mosaics to Impress

In this last section the techniques are still simple but are the ones that are often perceived as complicated. Once they are tried, it is liberating to discover how easy they are and how many ways they can be applied.

Wall Lizard

Direct method on net

The image of a lizard climbing up a wall brings
back hot vacations and so I've designed this
one to scurry up a post in the garden to
recreate that feeling. I have
made the design decorative
and glittery for the
same reason.

MATERIALS

Vitreous tiles, gold smalti (see color palette)

Glass beads or millefiori

Fiberboard (MDF) 17x13 inches

White paper for the design

Pencil

Sticky tape

Clear plastic or silicon-backed paper

Mesh

Trace down paper

Permanent marker

White craft glue (EVA) and brush

Nippers

Scissors

Quick-setting cement-based adhesive

Notched trowel

Wood block

Clean cloth

Sharp knife

Rubber gloves

Grout and squeegee

Tile cleaner

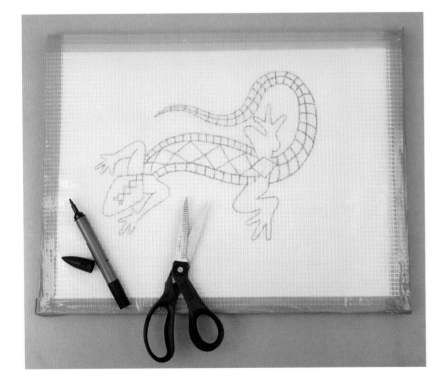

1. Draw the image on white paper and stick it to
the fiberboard with tape. Cover with a plastic
sheet to prevent the mosaic sticking to the
board and tape the mesh on top. Using a
permanent marker, trace the image onto the
mesh.

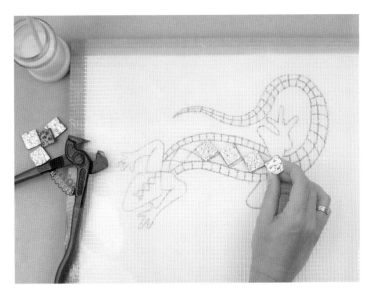

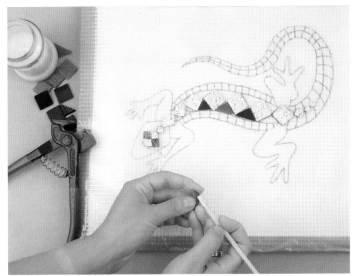

2. Starting with the diamonds on the lizards back, stick them to the mesh using the EVA using the direct method. The diamonds on the lizard's face are made using the reverse side of gold tiles.

3. Cut and stick the alternate triangles down both sides of the body and the tail.

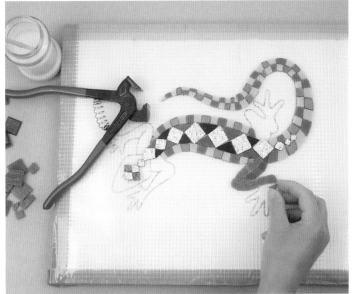

4. Stick alternate squares down the length of the body, placing upside-down gold tiles randomly.

5. Use two greens to fill in the lizard's legs.

6. Use beads or millefiori for the eyes, and place gold triangles to make the nose.

7. Complete the lizard by using light green tiles to make the face.

8. The lizard will be ready to transfer to the wall once the glue is dry.

9. When the glue is dry, remove the mosaic from the plastic and cut closely around the edge of the design. The lizard is now ready to fix to the wall.

10. Prepare the area of wall that the mosaic is to go on with a dilute solution of EVA and apply the cement based adhesive with a 1/8 inch notched trowel, making sure to push firmly against the wall to so that the right amount of adhesive is applied.

11. Place the mosaic onto the cement and, when it is in the correct position, gently press it into place using your hands or a wood block to ensure an even depth. The cement on the wall will come up through the mesh to hold the piece in place.

12. Clean off any excess from the sides or the surface with a knife or damp cloth. Keep the mosaic damp for 4–5 days with damp cloths then grout and clean following the instructions on pages 21–26.

Birdbath *Direct method*

Tiling the bottom of a pool or water feature has been used through history to both a practical and decorative effect. The glass tiles give a waterproof surface and glitter with the movement of the water in the sunlight. Projects like tiled swimming pools and water features are often very large and not many of us have enough space to accommodate them so, by covering a birdbath in mosaic, you can bring some of this beauty into your own garden however small.

NB. When using cement-based tile adhesive, read the instructions on the packet, which will dictate whether the glue can be applied to the tiles, to the surface of the birdbath, or to both. It can be easier to spread the adhesive onto the bird bath for larger areas but always "butter" smaller pieces of tile.

MATERIALS

Vitreous tiles, silver smalti, and mirror tiles

Millefiori or beads

Stone birdbath 14 inches diameter of bowl and

1.6 inch rim

White paper for the design

Pencil

Trace down paper

Permanent marker

Nippers

Tile adhesive (cement-based and waterproof)

Rubber gloves

Grout and squeegee

Clean cloth

Tile cleaner

1. Draw the image on white paper and transfer to the clean, dry birdbath using trace down paper. Reinforce the lines with the permanent marker.

2. Stick down the circles of colored tiles and the millefiori to form the scales of the first fish. Within this project there has been no attempt to make the shapes of the tiles represent scales or other parts of the body. It is a stylized design that gives the feeling of the fish without having to stick rigidly to form or color.

3. Cut and stick the long shapes for the tail and the underside fin.

4. Cut the triangles for the fin on top of the fish in the contrasting colors (see page 17) and stick them down.

5. Place the millefiori for the eyes of the first fish and place white tiles in a circle around them.

6. Place thin tiles to form the outline of the head and mouth.

7. Cut and stick down dark tiles for the inside of the mouth and pale tiles for the tongue.

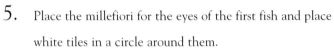

8. Fill in the tiles of the face, getting darker toward the edge.

9. Repeat the entire process for the second fish.

10. Stick the circular mirror tiles on to form the bubbles.

11. Use chalk to draw the movement of the water to a design you like, or by following the pattern in the template.

12. Complete the water area, using light and dark blue tiles getting lighter towards the edge to for the spray.

13. Lay tiles of blue and silver (or mirror tiles) around the top of the birdbath.

14. The birdbath is now ready to grout.

15. Grout and clean following the instructions on pages 21–26.

Snail Slab

Indirect method on paper

Creating a paving slab for the garden has some practical considerations as well as the creative ones. The slab must be structurally sound and the surface must be flat and made in a material that is both frost-proof and non-slippery. In order to make the slab completely flat, it is best to make the mosaic image using the indirect method and casting the concrete slab on top of it. Using glass tiles can cause problems in wet and icy weather, so I use predominantly frost-proof ceramic tiles.

MATERIALS

Ceramic tesserae (see color palette)

Wooden frame made of four 12.6 x 1.7 x 0.8 inches batons screwed onto a board 13.6 inches (see page 20)

Brown paper for the design

Scissors

Pencil

Trace down paper

Permanent marker

Nippers

White craft glue (PVA) watered down 50:50 and brush

Petroleum jelly

Rubber gloves

Grout

Cement

Sand

Trowel

Reinforcing wire

Wire cutters

Plastic sheeting and tape

Large board

Sponge

1. Cut the brown paper slightly smaller than the frame, draw out the image, and reinforce it with the permanent marker (working on the matte side of the paper).

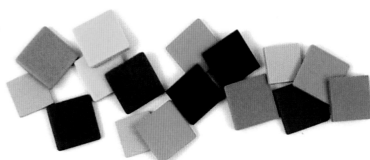

2. Using the black tiles, cut and stick the outline of the snail, remembering to place the tiles upside down.

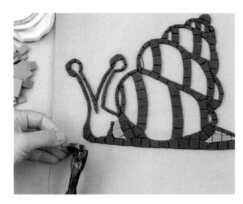

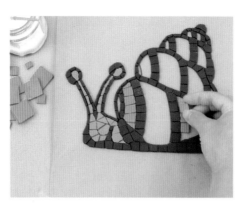

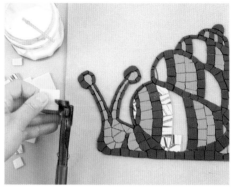

3. Cut the gray ceramic tiles to form the body of the snail.

4. Cut and stick the red tiles to the paper, fitting the tiles into the pattern created by the black outlines. This make of tiles has black lines on the back, but these will not show when the mosaic is reversed.

5. Add the yellow tiles to complete the snail.

6. Using a mixture of green tiles, cut random shapes and fill in the background.

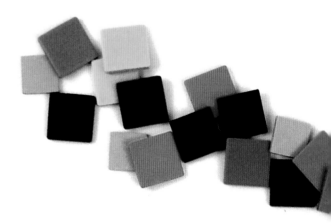

7. The finished image is now ready to pre-grout (see page 23).

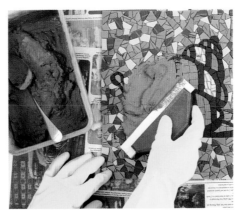

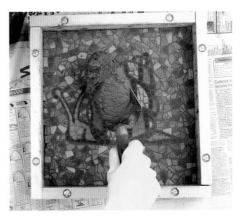

8. Sponge the petroleum jelly evenly over the inside of the frame. This will stop the slab sticking to the frame.

9. Mix a small quantity of grout and apply it to the back of the mosaic with a squeegee, pressing it into all the gaps between the tiles. This method ensures that there are no gaps under the tiles to weaken it. Remove any excess.

10. Place the mosaic, paper-side down into the frame. Mix up the concrete using one part cement to three parts sand, and add water slowly until it reaches a firm consistency. Trowel this onto the mosaic until it reaches half way up the frame and smooth it off.

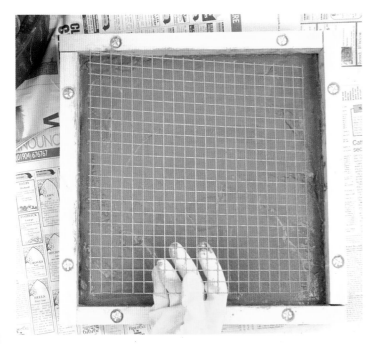

11. Cut the reinforcing wire to fit within the frame and place on top of the concrete. Add the rest of the mixture until it reaches the top of the frame. Now smooth it off using the trowel.

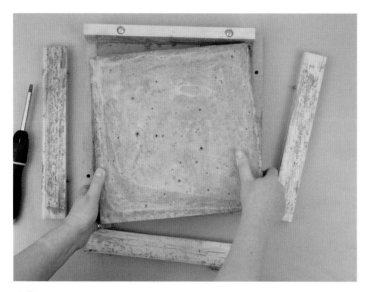

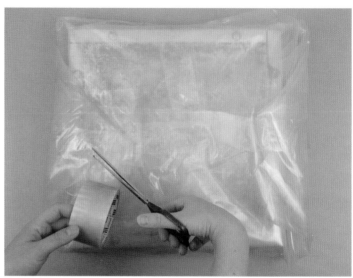

12. Remove each baton. Then placing a board on top of the mosaic turn, it over carefully to show the brown paper.

13. Wrap the slab in the plastic sheeting and leave it to dry for a week.

14. Wet the paper thoroughly with a sponge or cloth and leave for 15 minutes, making sure that it does not dry out. Peel the paper back from the edges carefully, remembering that the tiles on the edge of the mosaic are the most vulnerable. When the image is revealed, grout it with the same grout as before. Clean the grouted surface and then rewrap the slab for two weeks to allow it to dry completely. The slab is now finished and ready to be placed in the garden.

Elephant *Direct method*

This is the final project in the book and so I have enjoyed using different colors and textures to create a picture for the wall. The Indian running elephant is a favorite image of mine and I love the decoration of Indian art. The image in this piece is more complicated than in previous projects, but the techniques are no different. The only thing that makes it more of a challenge is the detail, which is much more time-consuming.

MATERIALS

Ceramic tiles, vitreous tesserae and gold smalti,
quarter black tiles (see color palette)

Thin tile edging

Beads, glass nuggets, and semi-precious stones

Metal and glass stars (backed with mock silver)

Plywood 17.2 x 26.8 inches

Batons 0.6 x 1.5 inches

Wood glue

White paper for the design

Pencil

Trace down paper

Permanent marker

Nippers

White craft glue (EVA) and brush

Silicone glue

Tile saw

1. I have used good-quality plywood but, owing to the weight of some of the materials, I have strengthened the back with batons to prevent the risk of warping.

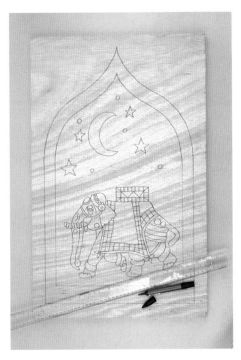

2. Draw the image on white paper and trace it down onto the plywood, reinforcing it with the permanent marker. Score the wood to enhance the adhesion.

3. Using the ceramic tiles, begin gluing them down for the elephant's blanket and top box.

4. Stick the tiles for the harnesses, edging, and ties on the elephant. There are no large areas of the same color on the image so it is better to start with the objects that would lie on top of the elephant. By getting these the right shape, you create a solid structure and then can fill in the white body.

5. Cut and stick the detailing of the eye and the headdress.

6. Cut the terracotta tiles carefully to make a smooth curve to the headdress.

  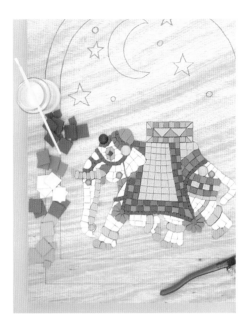

7.   Fill in all the remaining areas of the body with white. Cut and stick the tiles for
the grey toes.

8.   Working from the edge of the
board, stick the edging tiles down.
When they are cut make sure that
the ends that show are the glazed
ones. They can be cut with a tile
saw or nippers.

9. Stick the quarter black tiles around the inner edge of the arch. You can cut tiles into quarters for this but I have used pre-made quarter tiles because of their rounded surface and uniformity of shape.

10. Now infil the arch with a mixture of gold, beads and glass nuggets. By using small pieces of gold and interspersing them with other glittering objects less of the expensive gold is needed.

11. The different surfaces and detail in the found objects mixed with the gold creates a much richer and more luxurious look.

12. Using a mixture of greens and some semi-precious stones, make the grass for the elephant to walk on.

13. Choose some metal stars and stick them down. Cut some clear glass for the pinpoint lights and stick them down.

14. Stick down the clear glass stars and make the moon from gold tiles.

15. Cut a mixture of blue tiles for the sky and stick them with the lightest colors at the bottom getting darker toward the top.

16. Stick down the glass stars in the top two segments.

17. Surround the stars with the two dark blues and fill in the whole area. Once the glue is dry the elephant is ready to grout and clean following the instructions on pages 21–26.

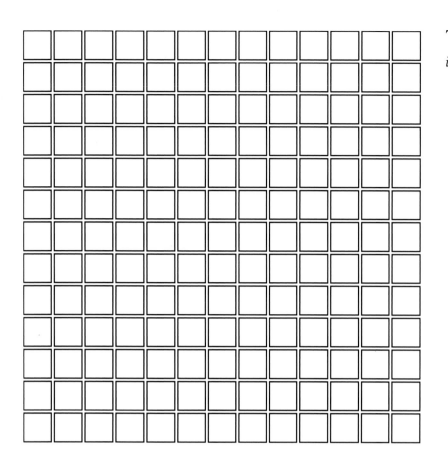

Trivet page 30
increase by 250%

Checkerboard page 33
increase by 500%

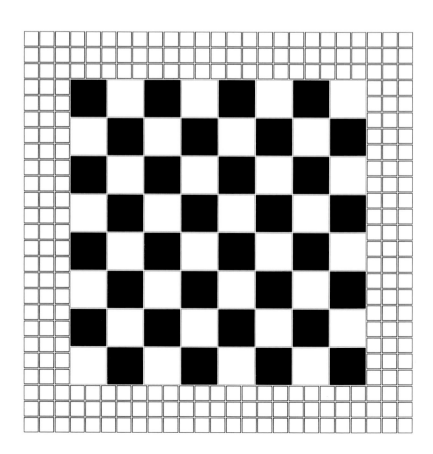

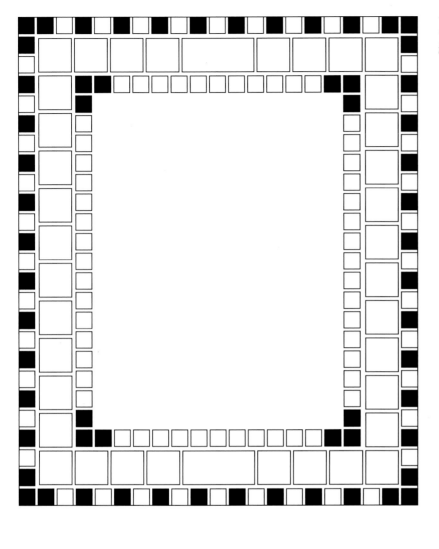

Picture Frame page 40
increase by 250%

0

1 2 3

4 5 6

7 8 9

House Number Plate
page 48

Fruit Bowl page 52
increase by 250%

Butterfly Table page 57
increase by 250%

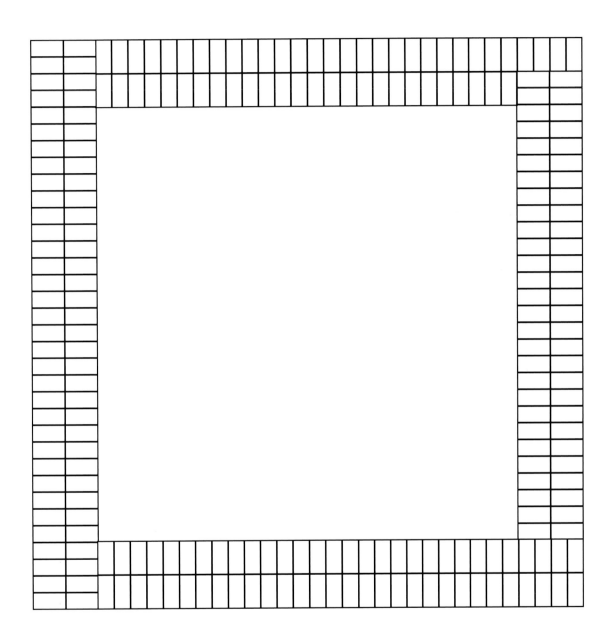

Mirror page 64
increase by 250%

Flying Bird Wall Plaque page 72
increase by 250%

Plant Pot with Ladybugs page 83

Wall Lizard page 90
increase by 200%

Birdbath page 95
increase by 225%

Snail Slab Page 101
increase by 141%

Elephant page 106
increase by 333%

Suppliers

Tiles that are suitable for mosaic work can be bought from a variety of places and do not have to be aquired from specialist shops. Local domestic tile warehouses and shops stock a range of tiles and accessories and have the advantage of being staffed by people who work in the tiling trade and are usually keen to share information. Tesserae and other small tiles are usually displayed in the shops but may need to be a special order. If it is proving difficult to find small tiles a swimming pool specialist will often either have stock or will be able to dirrect you towards a supplier. A good alternative is to look on the internet for mosaic associations such as the 'British Association for Modern Mosaic' or BAMM, and the 'Society of Americam Mosaic Artists'or SAMA. These sites are a great resource and will provide acess to suppliers and other help and contact that you may need.

The specialist mosaic suppliers listed below all stock a vast range of tiles and equipment. I have only indicated specific items that I have bought from them where I feel that it is difficult to get them elsewhere.

Paul Fricker Ltd
452 Pinhoe Road
Exeter EX4 8HN
01392 468 440

Mosaic Shop (small Indian mirror tiles in various shapes)
12/13 Pulteney Bridge
Bath BA2 4AY
01225 463 073

Mosaic Workshop   (Clock and table kits)
Unit B
443-449 Holloway Road
London N7 6LJ
0207 263 2997

Reed Harris Ltd
Riverside House
27 Carnwath Road
London SW6 3HR
0207 736 7511

Creative Beadcraft Ltd
Unit 2
Asheridge Business Centre
Asheridge Road
Chesham
Bucks HP5 2PT

House of Marbles   (Glass shapes)
Pottery Road
Bovey Tracey
Devon TQ13 9DS
01626 835285

James Hetley & Co Ltd
Glasshouse Fields
London E1W 3JA
0207 780 2343

Martin Cheek   (Millifiori)
Millifiori
Fkint House
21 Harbour Street
Broadstairs
Kent CT10 1ET
01843 861 958

Edgar Udny & Co Ltd
The Mosaic Centre
314 Balham High Road
London SW17 7AA
0208 767 8181

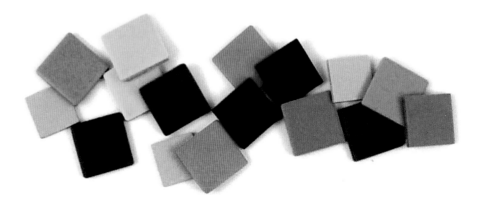

Glossary

Andamenti — The lines and direction of the tiles.

Buttering — Putting the adhesive directly onto the back of the tiles.

Casting — Making an object either with an integral mosaic surface like a slab or a solid object on which to add tiles.

Direct Method — Where mosaic is glued directly onto a surface in it's final postition with the tiles the correct way up.

Grout — The substance used to fill the gaps between the tiles.

Indirect method — Where the mosaic is temporarily stuck in reverse onto a surface before it is turned around and fixed into it's permenant position.

interstices — the spaces left between the tiles.

Nippers — An essential tool used to cut the tiles.

Opus — means the work. For some examples of various techniques see pages 24-25

Pre-grouting — This is a technique where the mosaic is grouted from the back in the reverse method befaore it is transfered to the final position.

Render — A smooth wall surface of sand and cement on which to fix a mosaic

Smalti — irregular pieces of hand cut enamelled glass which is left ungrouted

Tesserae — The tiles or objects used to make the mosaic

Vitreous glass — Square mosaic tiles made to a regular size and shape One side is smooth and the other is ridged for better adhesion.

Index

Credits and Acknowledgments

With love and thanks to Ned and Katy for their patience and understanding. Thanks also to Ned for his fanatastic design of this book, to Graham Price for his beautiful photographs and to Terry at Panache Studio for help with frames, advice and glass cutting lessons.

About the Author

Alison Hepburn was raised in the southeast of England, studying fine-art painting at St Albans and Exeter Colleges of Art. On graduation she returned to London, where she set up a graphic design and illustration business with Ned Hoste. She worked as an illustrator for 10 years, working on commissions for books, national magazines and newspapers, and greeting cards. While working as an illustrator, her work developed toward a highly decorative style, which led to her winning a commission from the National Silver Trust as part of a national competition in 1993.

Alison fulfilled a long-held ambition and took a course in mosaic, which led her to change career. She now works on private commissions and exhibitions and is a member of the British Association for Modern Mosaic. She lives in York with Ned and their daughter Katy.